This book belongs to

Leena the Detective

Five Pillars of Islam

DR. SAMRAH

AuthorHouse™
1663 Liberty Drive
Bloomington, IN 47403
www.authorhouse.com
Phone: 1 (800) 839-8640

Published by AuthorHouse 10/02/2019

ISBN: 978-1-7283-2171-4 (sc)
ISBN: 978-1-7283-2172-1 (e)

Library of Congress Control Number: 2019911001

Print information available on the last page.

Any people depicted in stock imagery provided by Getty Images are models,
and such images are being used for illustrative purposes only.
Certain stock imagery © Getty Images.

This book is printed on acid-free paper.

Because of the dynamic nature of the Internet, any web addresses or links contained in this book may have changed
since publication and may no longer be valid. The views expressed in this work are solely those of the author and do not
necessarily reflect the views of the publisher, and the publisher hereby disclaims any responsibility for them.

authorHOUSE®

In the name of Allah, Most Gracious, Most Merciful. To my kids, continue to be as happy and as God-fearing as you are today. For my wonderful husband, parents, and siblings, thank you for your great support in writing this book, and for your everlasting love. To all the young readers, this is for you.

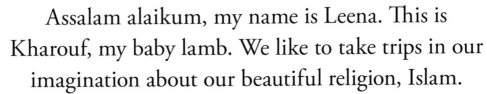

Assalam alaikum, my name is Leena. This is Kharouf, my baby lamb. We like to take trips in our imagination about our beautiful religion, Islam.

We also love to explore new things to improve our understanding of Islam, says Kharouf. My mom gave me this camera, says Leena. As soon as you say Bismillah incredible things happen.

Our imagination will help us learn, says Kharouf. Let's explore our imagination for the five pillars of Islam, the actions of all Muslims around the world!", exclaims Leena excitedly.

"Bismillah, bismillah, bismillah! Let's learn about the five pillars of Islam." says Leena.

لَآ اِلٰهَ اِلَّا اللّٰهُ مُحَمَّدٌ رَسَوْلُ اللّٰهِ

"Kharouf, we have come to the first pillar of Islam!"says
Leena. The first pillar of Islam is the Shahadah. Muslims
declare that there is only one God and that Mohamed
(peace be upon him) is our final prophet, says Kharouf

The second pillar of Islam is salah. God requires all Muslim to perform five daily prayers, says Kharouf. The five daily prayers are Fajr (morning), dhuhr(noon), asr (afternoon), maghrib (sunset), and isha (night).

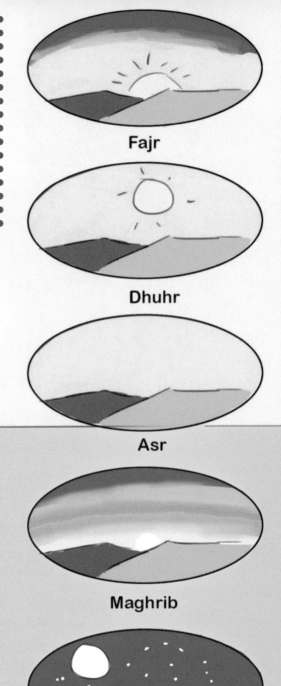

Fajr

Dhuhr

Asr

Maghrib

Isha

The third pillar of Islam is Zakat. As Muslims, we give our earnings to the needy.

The fourth pillar of Islam is sawm. In the month of Ramadan, we fast from dawn until sunset, says Leena. We will also enjoy iftar with our family and friends, says Kharouf.

The fifth pillar of Islam is Hajj. Hajj is done in the holy land of Makkah, Saudi Arabia, says Kharouf. Every Muslim dreams to go there!, says Leena.

"So Kharouf we saw all of the five pillars. Can you name them now?"asks Leena. "Yes, it's shahadah, salah, zakat, sawm, and of course hajj."remembers Kharouf. "Mumtaz!" says Leena excitedly.

Well done top detective

It was so easy to learn the five pillars of Islam. We learned the different acts of a Muslims just by saying Bismillah.

"What a journey it was." says Leena. "That was fun!" says Kharouf.
We hope to see you on our next adventure, insha'Allah.

Dr. Samrah is an American born Muslim.
This is her first book of a series of books. Recently, she was inspired by the children she works with. She offers her eloquent storytelling in return for smiles. She was encouraged by those children to write her first book targeted to young Muslims. Prior to that, she spent years studying various children's Islamic books and received a lot of her inspiration from childhood experiences and her love for reading. She is a mother of two amazing kids and lives her life to assure that they get the best in this world and work hard with them to succeed in the hereafter. Allah knows best.

"As a Muslim and a mom, I wanted a book that would make learning about Islam fun and interactive for young readers. Leena reminds me of my daughter, who is always inquisitive, my little detective. She is also like my son, who always finds a way to make the world make sense. All of my kids are an inspiration for this book."

Dr. Samrah

Glossary of terms:
Bismillah- In the name of God
Allah- Arabic word for God
Asslam alaikum- peace be with you
Islam- submission to God
Mumtaz- Arabic word for excellent
Shahadah- statement of the Islamic faith
Salah- prayer
Zakat- giving to the poor
Sawm- fasting
Iftar- break fast
Hajj- pilgrimage

Printed in the United States
By Bookmasters